Broken Yet Not Defeated

Jeffrey Brian Sullivan

ISBN 979-8-89485-043-6 (Paperback)
ISBN 979-8-89485-044-3 (Digital)

Covenant Books
11661 Hwy 707
Murrells Inlet, SC 29576
www.covenantbooks.com

INTRODUCTION

At forty-seven years old, I, Jeffrey Brian Sullivan, chronicle my desperate struggle to treat my sudden diagnosis of brain, lymph-node, and stomach metastasized lung cancer. In a desperate attempt to live despite a dire, imminent, terminal stage-four diagnosis with only days or weeks left, I share my five-year journey to defeat the odds for myself and others to come. I've braved through highly experimental brain treatments and debili-tating regular chemo treatments to the max, and my determination and desire to live shine through.

In October 2018, my life, career, and future came to a sudden and crashing halt. With only hours to attempt to save my life and dreams, I consented to what would be the fight for my life, led by my dedicated oncologist through this crisis. With my family, friends, and employer urging me on, read about my battle to beat all odds and survive.

CHAPTER 1

April of 2018 I began to have a terrible cough and would choke in the early mornings.

Signs of cancer I overlooked

I have smoked for so many years that I just figure it is smoker's cough, but I also have reflux acid that is yellow in color coming up. I just deal with it and keep on going as I always do. By changing my eating habits, it gets a little better. I am working five to six days a week out of town, trying to get all things caught up on my to-do list of personal business and my daily duties for my job.

I'm a contractor and travel between three different states in the southeastern US, driving an 18-wheeler two or three days a week, and I am burning the candle at both ends for several months. After losing my dad in 2011 and then my mom in 2017, I've just buried all my energy in working. Working helps me deal with the terrible, empty, and heart-wrenching pain of not being able to speak with either of my parents anymore on the phone or in any other way.

Finally, a much-needed vacation arrives in my schedule. I now have twelve full days and nights to do whatever I desire without worry and quickly plan a trip to the Kentucky Derby and then immediately afterward to Florida for eight days.

This week, I drive 2,300 miles in an 18-wheeler, then get right back on the road to go to the Kentucky Derby. Derinda and I arrive at Churchill Downs track. We have never been to this type of event. It is a very big deal, with what looks like hundreds of thousands of people and their cars, trucks, vans, buses, and limousines all in attendance without anywhere to park them. I have to park some four miles from the track, at a beautiful and very old church. There, the Boy Scouts, Troop 317, of Lexington, Kentucky, ask for $5. I pay it plus $10 for the boys to get themselves some Cokes and hot dogs for lunch from the little store beside the church.

Being an ex–Boy Scout myself, it is just my choice. I feel that if I park my truck closer in someone's yard, I do not know from a hole in the ground for $150 that my truck will either get run into, vandalized, or even worse, stolen while we are at the Derby. The Boy Scout church lot just seems a much smarter choice. We are able to get a free shuttle car ride back to the racetrack. I tip the driver $5.

Wow! In shock and awe, Derinda and I feel really out of place with all these yuppies and rich elitists. We are almost disgusted enough to just leave and not even stay for the race. Then the rain sets in. All the uncovered outdoor seats the rich people paid for have nobody sitting in them. Derby rules do not let you have your umbrella and make you leave it at the entry gates. So I give Derinda my old cowboy hat and find a trash bag. I clean it really well while standing in the rain and make myself a poncho out of it.

Feeling snubbed, I tell Derinda, "Hold my hand. We are gonna plow through these intoxicated people, march right out there in the rain, sit in their expensive paid-for seats they ain't sitting in, and watch these horses run these races."

The seats are trackside at Turn 3. I get dirt thrown in my face by horses kicking it up as they run by. In my opinion, they are the best seats in the whole darn place. So we make the best of what we can get out of the $160 tickets that just get us in but do not get us a seat or even allow us to see the racetrack. I guess you could say I am not going to put up with this nonsense, and I just kinda make my own rules.

We have a great time even though it rains for seven straight hours. (American Pharoah is the Derby winner and even goes on to become the Triple Crown winner that year. He is so amazing to watch in real time. *Hell!* He even kicked mud on me as he went by. I don't think you can get much closer to the horses than that unless you are on one of them. Absolutely great race. Now it is time to leave, and *so it begins.*

I am walking and walking—no shuttles to get you back to your car. It is torrentially downpouring, and we are cold and soaked to the bone. Our phones will not get a GPS signal, so now we are lost. The area surrounding the Derby is very, very rough, unsafe, and strewn with Third World–type housing projects. I have no kind of weapon. She is scared. I am as well but can't let her see it. All of a sudden, I have an extremely sharp, stabbing pain in my left side, deep within my body. It stops me in my tracks.

She asks, "What's wrong?"

I reply, "I don't know, but, man, this hurts."

Now my whole left leg will not even move right. It is not a stroke, and it is not a pain in my heart or my back. I believe that at this very moment, the tumor in my left lung begins to grow and lets me know it is in me.

I look to Derinda and say, "See the police? I am going to talk to them and see if they can help us get on the right road to finding the church we parked at."

We have been walking for over two hours at this point. Finally, one policeman gets a signal on his computer in the cruiser and points us in the right direction.

After two and a quarter miles more of walking, we eventually arrive at the church and get in the truck. Both she and I are soaked, tired, cold, and starving. I don't dare tell her just how bad I'm really hurting, so I begin the journey back. We decide to just head to Florida and not go back by the house, which would be a longer detour. I drive from Kentucky to our North Georgia camper and lot in the Ellijay Mountains for the night to rest and then head to Florida. I know something is definitely wrong in my body, but I never in a million years would have thought it is cancer.

Awaking in the mountains

We awake to a beautiful day in the mountains of Ellijay, see the deer, have coffee, and get all the items on my "Leaving the Camper Checklist" done before beginning our journey to Florida. I have now driven across five states in the last twenty-four hours and am about to do two more. The pain in my chest is constant now, and my left leg from the hip down is really in a lot of pain. I know I am not well but feel like I do not want to mess up our vacation. We have waited over two years to take some time together, and she needs this as much as I do.

It is a beautiful day—no rain expected for the next seven days. It's going to be a beautiful and fun-packed trip. We stop in Alabama, at a Cracker Barrel restaurant we like, eat a good lunch, and discuss what we are going to do for the next few days. I know we are going to visit some nice restaurants in Pensacola, Florida, and do some fishing, sightseeing, and lots of *shopping*.

We arrive at our hotel, and the place is absolutely amazing. The location on the bay is awesome, and I wish I had chosen this place years ago. It is now 6:00 PM, and we are tired. However, we walk out to the beach and sit to watch the beautiful sunset.

Derinda asks me if I am okay.

I say, "Yes," but I am really hurting and having trouble breathing as well as swallowing when I drink or eat.

We are thrilled over how perfect the hotel is. After a few hours of romantic bayside lounging, stargazing, and a few good kisses, we decide to turn in. I notice I am unable to lie on my right side in bed. I have to lie on my left, or I can't breathe. This is a serious issue, but I still just push it to the side and keep on going. I fall fast asleep and get some much-needed rest.

I am so tired from driving across seven states that I sleep in late. Derinda actually wakes me with breakfast in bed—so sweet. I am shocked it is almost 9:00 AM; I never sleep past 6:00 AM. This is also a sign my body is in trauma. I just don't realize it because I am not thinking about having cancer at all. I get up and shower; and we begin our sightseeing and shopping, enjoying our day.

We find this park not far from the hotel where some of the oldest known living live oak trees in the US are located. We walk through the walking paths and see a lot of birds and really awesome old trees. I notice that walking for any length of time is becoming a real challenge to me and my breathing; I have to stop a lot. I see that she is worried, so I tell her all of what I have been feeling. Now she is mad at me for not telling her sooner. I assure her I am okay, that it will be all right once I get all this rest and have no work for the next eight days and that I will begin to feel better.

This vacation is basically all spent eating at fine restaurants, fishing as much as we can, and enjoying the pool and beach as much as possible. We eat at Saltgrass Steak House on the Bay. I am very impressed with the quality of service, and the food is the best out-to-eat experience I have had in a long time. I am going to really miss the tranquility of being able to sleep, eat, fish, and sit by the ocean as well as walk in one place without ever having to crank the car and drive anywhere. This is by far the best vacation I have ever had. Planning it in advance was a good thing.

Now we have to pack it up and head back to our everyday normal working lifestyle, just working our life away. I get all the stuff and head down the stairs four times. The pain in my lung hits me again suddenly, this time very intense, and I just *stop*. I am now breathing short and coughing up yellow mucus. Derinda comes around the corner, sees me bent over coughing, and gets really upset. I wish she had not seen this, but I can't hide it. Now we know something is up. I tell her that I will make an appointment for a full physical and see what's up. We begin the seven-hour trip back home. Arriving home, we get unpacked, eat a light dinner, and turn in for the evening.

CHAPTER 2

Back to my working life

It's the month of July, and we have just one day of vacation left, which we spend at home cleaning the house, cutting the grass and watching NASCAR races on TV.

I send out an email about my expected duties for the next week. My boss replies right away, telling me to come to the office because we need to load the big truck and make several runs to South Carolina this week. We watch old Westerns on TV, eat a good home-cooked meal, and go to bed.

We awake; and I get a shower, shave, brush my teeth, eat a bowl of oatmeal, drink two cups of coffee, pack my travel bag, take my meds, and rush out the door to the pickup truck. Derinda pretty much does the same routine, then rushes out the door to her old red F150 pickup truck and heads to work.

I am in McDonough, Georgia, now loading two Bobcat S650 tractors on the trailer along with several pallets of floor and wall tile. This load will be delivered to three different locations: Orangeburg, South Carolina; Cayce, South Carolina; and Charleston, South Carolina. Then I pick up the tile and another tractor here. I make the drop and the pickup and head to Orangeburg, South Carolina. I check into a room at Comfort Inn, then grab a bite to eat at Bojangles—chicken and rice, half and half—and tea to drink. I walk back to the room, watch the news, make calls, send out the end-of-day progress report, and go to bed. I do not sleep well this night as my legs are really sore. This is a new ache that I have not had before. I rub some muscle rub on my calf muscles and try to sleep.

After a restless night of not getting much quality sleep, I get up, shower, brush my teeth, take my meds, and head down to the first floor to eat breakfast and check out. I get to the truck, start to climb up, and have a little difficulty climbing the three steps into the rig. I do my logbook while the truck warms up, then get ready to begin the day heading to my last drop of this trip to Augusta, Georgia.

I get on Highway 601, take it to Highway 178, and then merge into Interstate 20 West. I now have sharp pains in my legs and feet, making it very difficult to push the clutch in and shift gears in this big truck. I take a couple of Motrin and just push on in pain. I arrive in Augusta, Georgia, at Washington Road, at a McDonald's Restaurant. This is a very busy location and hard to get into with this big truck, but I do get unloaded. This is going to be my next eight-week project, an MRP (major remodel project), which will include new drive-through (DT) order points and a PlayPlace unit, as well as a new roof and a complete demo of the exterior mansard roof with a flat roof on the top of the building.

I get back into the truck. I had gotten rained on while unloading and am a little wet, but it does not seem too bad. I update my logbook and begin to head back to McDonough, Georgia.

Arriving in McDonough

I am now back on the road and should arrive in McDonough at about 6:00 PM. I will get out of the truck and then have to jump in my pickup truck to head home for the night. I will next stop at exit 138 on Interstate 20 West, a Flying J truck stop, and put fuel in the truck.

I am making good time; there's not too much traffic out here this time of day—no rain and a smooth ride. I arrive at the fuel stop, pull up to the pumps, and shut off the rig. I open the door and notice a sharp pain in my lower back, on the left side. It is very painful as I climb down out of the truck.

I undo the fuel-tank cap on the driver's-side tank, insert the pump, walk around to the passenger side pump, undo the fuel-tank cap, and insert that pump. The truck holds one hundred gallons of diesel fuel. It takes about ten minutes to fill both tanks. I finally get all the fuel and head into the station to get a copy of my receipt and a cold drink.

While waiting in line, my back hurts badly when I reach behind to get my wallet out of my back pocket. The pain takes my breath away; it's very painful. I pay for my drink, get my fuel ticket, and head back out to my truck. I get back up in the truck. Now I am just in a lot of pain and still have to drive another seventy miles to the shop and then seventy-four miles to get home. *This is gonna be awful!* I think.

I finally arrive at home. I call Derinda and tell her, "I need help getting out of the truck and into the house."

She comes out to the driveway, assists me, and notices I am breathing heavily.

I say, "Yes, I am in a lot of pain, and breathing is difficult." I have an appointment next weekend with CVS pharmacy to do a full physical to renew my medical card; maybe I will find out what's going on. I tell Derinda, "Don't worry. I am going to call the doctor to make an appointment for me to see him."

We eat dinner, watch a little TV, and go to bed.

I have to sleep on my right side; it is far too painful to sleep any other way, which is not how I normally sleep. For now, it's what I have to do. I am hurting so badly that getting to sleep is difficult, but I finally fall asleep around 1:00 AM.

I get up at 6:45 AM. She ask how I am feeling, as she always does, and I reply, "A little better, not hurting badly anymore." We both think maybe I have just pulled a muscle in my back. I kiss her goodbye and head off to work.

I have to go to the shop today and work there all day. I am cleaning up the equipment, staging arcas for materials, and organizing all the tile and grout inside the shop. I do all my work and don't have a lot of pain, but I do have a cough that just will not go away. I finally finish for the day and head home. TGIF.

I get home before Derinda, make a pot of coffee, and lie down to rest on the couch. I feel so tired; it's been a long, hard week. I have to go to an appointment early in the morning, so we just eat dinner and watch old Westerns on TV. I actually fall fast asleep on the couch. She just covers me up and lets me be.

I am now back on I-20 eastbound, headed back to the shop, a 127-mile trip. I arrive in McDonough, Georgia, and park the big truck. I notice that my legs are very numb, more so than normal after driving for two days. I manage to get up out of the seat, holding the steering wheel and door. I push myself up, grab the handles on the side of the cab, and begin to climb down to the ground. My legs are very weak, and it is challenging to just walk to my pickup truck. I finally get situated in my truck and head home to Paulding County, Georgia.

Home at last, I am now in so much pain in my legs that I am unable to walk on my own. I text Derinda to come down and help. Together we manage to get all 277 pounds of me into the house and up the stairs. I sit down at the kitchen table and get my work boots off my extremely swollen feet and then eat a good dinner, which she prepared for us.

While eating, she asks, "What is wrong?"

I say, "I really don't know. My legs are just starting to become very weak. I'm not sure what is going on."

I rest all weekend, staying off my feet as much as possible.

Monday morning
Mid-September 2018

It's a big day today: I start the demolition process of my project. I get up at 4:00 AM, shower, and take my daily meds. I load all my stuff into the truck for the next five days out of town. I am now on my way to Washington Road in Augusta, Georgia.

I arrive first on-site, get my plans out, and wait for my subcontractors' arrivals. I am expecting plumbers, electricians, and framers today. We are to close the lobby and begin exterior demo today and interior demo tomorrow. They all show up by 9:00 AM and complete their parts by the end of the day. The exterior demo roof will take eight days—demo and rebuild as we go. Electrical lights, interior and building exterior, are all being demoed back to junction boxes as these circuits will be reused.

I am tired. After a long day, at 7:00 PM, I decide to go to my hotel in Aiken, South Carolina, at exit 5, 120 West Sleep Inn. I notice my legs are swollen badly again. I take aspirin, eat a burger, watch the weather, and go to bed.

I sleep very well this night and feel refreshed when I wake up. There's no pain in my legs, the swelling is gone, and I feel good. I get showered, brush my teeth, get dressed, go to the lobby, eat breakfast, drink apple juice, and grab a small coffee. Then I head to the jobsite.

CHAPTER 3

Entering scary uncertainties

I am now at my appointment for a full certified-driver DOT physical. I am the only person in line at CVS Pharmacy in Hiram, Georgia.

The nurse opens the door and says, "I am sorry, Mr. Sullivan. I am unable to do this due to my certification renewal not being complete yet."

I say, "Okay, so where can I go now and get it done?"

She calls Austell, Georgia, and checks to see if the nurse on duty there has a current DOT certification number to perform the exam.

I am now en route to the CVS Pharmacy in Austell, Georgia. It's a beautiful day, and I am driving my Dodge Charger SRT today. It is very fun to drive, but unfortunately, I don't get to drive it much. Today is a good day for it. I arrive and am behind five people; it's going to be a long wait. I just sit and look at my phone for what seems like forever.

Finally, after two hours, it's my turn to see the nurse. I enter the little five-by-twelve-foot room. It's a very young nurse. She tells me I am the second person she's had to do a DOT physical since she got her certification.

I think, *Oh* crap, *she is gonna do everything absolutely by the book. I am in for it.*

"It" begins. Blood is drawn, blood pressure is checked, and vitals are checked. I lie down on the exam table. She pushes on my sternum area and says she feels something that could be a hernia. It is tender, but I don't dare flinch. I need to pass this exam today because my CDL license is up for renewal in three days.

She tells me to sit up, then checks my reflexes and measures my neck size. Now we do the eye exam. Oddly enough, I pass the eye exam without using my reading glasses. Now the pharmacist is in the room. I have to take off my shorts so she can check for hernias. I turn my head and cough, and all is good. They are not allowed to be alone in the room while they do this test, so the pharmacist is there just for protocol.

It is time for the hearing test. This is what I always worry about. I hear the fluorescent lights blasting a loud humming noise, as well as the music playing rather loudly inside CVS, and so she starts to whisper. I can't hear a darn thing she says. I complain that this is not a totally quiet area. I am a little hard of hearing in one ear, but this place has the music up too loud. Also, the light in this room needs the ballast replaced. That is what the constant humming is that even she can hear.

She says, "Let's turn off the light and try again."

I still can't hear a darn thing she whispers, so I fail my physical and am only given a three-month medical card.

She tells me I have ninety days from today to get a true hearing test and a letter from my primary doctor saying I do not have a hernia in my chest. I pay $159 and leave. I am absolutely ticked off about this. I will call my doctor on Monday morning and see if he will write me a letter and tell me where to go to get a hearing test.

I get in my car and drive back home, thinking this is going to cost me a whole bunch of money. I know I'm pretty deaf in my left ear, but now it is both ears. And that place where she pushed on my chest is very sore. I hope she is wrong about the hernia.

Well, it's my birthday now. I have found out I am basically deaf and may have another hernia. I am forty-seven today and think, *Gosh, it sure isn't fun growing old.* I get tired very fast now and don't have nearly the same amount of energy I had in my twenties and thirties. I seem to be going to doctors more and more and am on five different daily medications.

I make the appointment to see an audiologist. The hearing exam is going to cost me $554. I do not have insurance, so I just have to bite the bullet and pay it.

Derinda tells me we are going to be able to get insurance soon with her new job, but she is not sure if she wants to get it.

I say, "Please get it and get the best plan they have to offer. I don't care how much it costs. I will pay for it."

Derinda says, "Okay, I will get it once they let me."

I call my primary care doctor to see if he will just write me a letter stating that I don't have a hernia. He will not do it and says I will need to see him first. I make an appointment with him for the same day as the hearing test. This will cost me another $150. This darn yearly medical card required for CDL drivers is gonna be super expensive for me to obtain my one-year card this year. My appointments are for September 24, 2018. I guess that day, I will find out a lot about myself.

I continue on with my normal everyday lifestyle, working all the time. I am now starting a new project in Augusta, Georgia. I will be doing a full remodel on the Washington Road McDonald's. This project was put on hold earlier this year, and now, finally, I get to do it. I am delivering a lot of materials to this jobsite as well as many others in South Carolina. My project start date is September 27, 2018. I am looking forward to being in one place for a few weeks and not having to drive so much, especially in the 18-wheeler, as it's becoming a real challenge for me to get in and out of that big truck, push the clutch, and shift the gears constantly.

September 24, 2018

I get up, shower, shave, brush my teeth, and then go to my hearing test appointment.

I am placed in a soundproof room, which was just built at the doctor's office and has the latest state-of-the-art hearing test equipment. The doctor gives me instructions on what to do with a button, places headphones on my ears, and then leaves the room.

The test begins with my left ear first, with a full array of sounds, dings, pings, and thunks. The sounds are all at various decibel levels, and I have to push the button when I am capable of hearing the sounds. This lasts about four minutes per ear. Each ear, right and left, is subjected to the exact same dings, pings, and thunks. I am confident I am doing really well on this portion of the test.

This part of the test is complete.

Through the headphones, the doctor says, "Now we are going to speak solitary words in your left ear first and right ear last." These words will all be of similar sound, using different vowels and consonants in very similar words, all spoken at different decibel levels of sound. "When you hear the word, you speak into a microphone what word you heard."

I do this for about four minutes per ear. I am also very confident I am doing really well on this portion of my hearing test.

The doctor says through the earphones that now we will do some tests of very high-pitched sounds in each ear and instructs me to push the button when I hear the sound clearly and certainly when I know that I heard something. This frequency level of sound will be so high you would not hear it at first. A dog would hear this frequency before any human ever would, but as it emits a frequency level you can detect, hit the button. I believe I do well on this test also.

I am now out of the soundproof booth and in the results room. The doctor shows me my results on all the different tests. I am literally shocked at what I am seeing. Not only did I fail, but I failed all tests very badly. I find out I have 60 percent hearing loss in my right ear and 80 percent in my left ear. The doctor recommends that I consider hearing aids for both ears. I ask how much they are. I am told a price, and again, I am shocked.

I tell the doctor, "Thank you, but at this time, this old cowboy is a poor man and uninsured. So the hearing aids will have to wait." I then show the doctor this knot that has suddenly developed under my right ear just in the last two weeks. I get concerned when, after he checks it, he says, "We need to schedule you for a CT scan."

I ask why he is concerned.

He says that it is a tumor but not to worry, as it's very common in men and is almost always benign.

I am now scared, concerned, and very worried about myself. I tell the doctor I should have some insurance in two weeks and ask if we can schedule the CT scan for the first week in October.

He says, "Sure," and that he would like to get the results of the scan and then do a follow-up based on the results.

I say, "Okay."

I leave this doctor and head to my primary doctor for my appointment with him to do my blood work panel and basic checkup, which he does about every four months. Since I am diabetic, the doctor has to renew my scripts for all my related medications. I have a very *cool* doctor. He is ex-Navy and also a very avid canvas painter. I have been seeing him now for six years or so. Very good guy.

The nurses do all the routine stuff and tell me the doc will be in shortly. I feel this knot under my ear. It does not hurt, but it is definitely getting bigger.

The doctor comes into the room, and the first thing he says after checking my neck is "Wow, what's that? How long has it been there?"

I ask, "What?"

"The little knot on your neck.

"My neck? Where?"

My doctor puts his finger on the left side of my neck, and sure enough, I feel a knot there as well. I did not notice this myself just three hours ago when I was in my bathroom shaving. I then tell him to look at the knot under my right ear.

The doctor says, "Crap! We got to get you scheduled for a CT scan immediately."

I say, "*Okay*, the hearing doctor is also concerned about this. He is scheduling a CT scan for the neck up with and without contrast for the first week of October. I will finally have some health insurance again by then."

My doctor is very glad to hear the news of my new insurance. He then tells me he wants the CT scan with and without contrast from the chin down to below the abdominal area. The doc also checks me for a hernia in my chest and says I am good there. Then he says, "Jeff, I am concerned about these knots. We need to do a follow-up immediately following the results of the scans."

I say, "Okay, the hearing doctor said the same thing this morning and also said this one under my ear is a tumor and instructed me not to worry. It's relatively common in men my age but is almost always benign."

My doctor says, "I agree with him, but the sudden swelling of the knot in your neck and the lymph nodes, along with the absence of an earache, sore throat, or flu, is very alarming. Let's get the scans and go from there."

I get my meds rescripted for six months, leave the doctor's office, and then return home. I stop at the Sunoco gas station near my home in Dallas, Georgia, to get some lunch from the kitchen there. They have great chicken wings and fingers, taters, and rolls. I leave the station, head to the house, eat my lunch there, and then try to absorb all this very scary info my two doctors have just given me. I can say now that I am extremely worried, and even worse, I now have to figure out how to tell Derinda without totally scaring the heck out of her.

Tomorrow I will return to work. I have a lot of driving to do this week to get materials. I have to get tractors and other equipment moved from Georgia to South Carolina and meet my boss and the McDonald's owner and construction manager at my project on Friday at 11:00 PM. I decide that I will not tell Derinda just yet. I will think about it this week while I am driving and then tell her over the weekend so as not to worry her about me just yet. There really is no good way to break this terrible news to her, as she loves and depends on me completely. This is going to worry her deeply. I will figure out a way to tell her in a softer way than the doctors just plainly gave it to me. I am glad my doctors realize I am a man and expect them to be straight up with me and tell me like it is without *sugarcoating it*. I do, however, want to tell all who read this that I just got what I consider to be the harshest and most alarming information about my health I have ever received in my life.

I am very truly scared.

CHAPTER 4

Rapid speech and mobility issues

I am working on my project in Augusta, Georgia, on Washington Road. This is a place in my life I will never forget. I begin the project with the exterior demo of the building, the roof mansard, and the parking lot. This is a remove-and-reframe-as-you-go process. The parking lot demo involves removing, regrading, and placing and finishing new concrete as you go as well. My crews are working hard every day; we all have a lot to do and a six-week deadline to meet.

The drive-through at this store remains open the entire time we are under construction. This is a tough task as you are always confronted with safety concerns and lines of cars waiting to pull to the window, pay, get food, and go. You have to maintain clean drive-through lanes, free of all screws, nails, and demo debris, and make sure you do not crush cars or people as you take off large sections of the building. Having been doing jobs like this for over twenty years, I have grown accustomed to it, as have my men who are working on the job. My boss has always paid me and the subcontractors well to take care of his needs as well as McDonald's needs during construction, so we all make a great team.

This process takes about two and a half weeks and is hard work from daylight to dark every day. During these two and a half weeks, I also contact several materials suppliers and coordinate the delivery of new materials for the construction of new buildings. This part of my job is very physical. When the materials arrive, I have to handle unloading them with an off-road forklift and a tractor with forks. I have pallets of heavy tile and mortar that have to be staged out of the way, quantified, back-checked with order and ship tickets, then covered and protected from the elements.

I also have lots of heavy items that go into a forty-foot-long storage container and a twenty-foot storage container. All the items inside the building's lobby and front counter area go into the forty-foot container, as do some of my new construction materials. All the items placed into the twenty-foot box, which I have to take off trucks, break down pallets of lights, bathroom fixtures, doors, frames, all restroom accessories, and many other expensive new items. I pick up these items one by one and place them into the trailer in an organized manner to get at the stuff needed efficiently during the new build-out.

I am starting to notice that as I pick up things to hand-carry them into the storage containers, I am coughing every time I bend over and pick up anything. It's a cough that really hurts deep inside my chest. I am having a slightly difficult time bending down and getting back upright. Just walking is becoming extremely painful.

I am now growing concerned. The CT scan results came back a week ago. My doctor said they showed what is consistent with lymphoma cancer. I have not wanted to accept this as correct and have been working through it, hoping that his diagnosis is wrong and that I will get better. I have not told anyone what the doctor said. I do know my body is hurting terribly, and I am really struggling to breathe at night when I am trying to sleep.

Thursday
October 25, 2018

I am almost done with the project, and I am not well. I now cannot get on my knees and get back up without help. I am losing weight very quickly, not eating like normal, and feeling very tired all day. I am losing my voice and truly cannot talk. It is very painful to talk, and people are having difficulty understanding what I am saying, especially on the phone.

I tell the owner of the store and my boss that I am going to go to the STAT Clinic at Kennestone Hospital on October 29, 2018. I get through this week, getting all the items related to the project out of my truck, including blueprints and keys to trailers, and put them inside the twenty-foot container. I then load up my tools and my tool trailer and get ready to go home. My friends and coworkers are all worried about me. I am not well at all.

5:00 AM
October 26, 2018

This morning, at the hotel, I cannot physically get out of bed, put my pants on, or put on my boots. I am in serious trouble. I have to call the front desk. Mr. David, a man I have known for four years now, who also knows I am not well, agrees to come to my room and help me. Thank God he agreed to do so. He helps me get dressed, gets my clothes and extra stuff out of the room, and helps me to my truck. I head to work.

When I get to the jobsite, my coworker and longtime friend, Roberto, is already on-site. I sit in my truck until he walks over. I can hardly speak and am not able to move my legs well at all. However, if someone helps me out of the truck, I can walk with my cane. He helps me out, and I begin what is to be my hardest day of work ever. I can only tell people what to do by typing it on my phone and texting answers to their questions because I have lost my voice.

I finish up my day at the jobsite. I tell the owner and all my subs goodbye and get my friend Roberto to help me into my truck. I head home. It takes me four hours; traffic is really bad today in Atlanta.

During my trip home, my legs go completely numb. I really have no idea how I am going to get into my house once I get home. Finally, I arrive. Derinda comes outside to greet me as usual. She gets my stuff and starts taking it into the house. I just sit there in the truck because I really cannot move my legs at all on my own now, and I cannot talk either.

She comes back out in a few minutes, saying, "Come on, let's get you out and into the house."

I just sit there with tears in my eyes as I can hear her just fine. I just can't tell her I am paralyzed from the waist down. I begin to cry because I really don't know what to do. Derinda then realizes I am not able to move. Now she is upset, very scared, and worried. I put her hands on my legs to steady them because I am able to move my arms, and then I push my legs out of the truck. She helps me position my legs so I can slide out of the truck. My legs are so weak now that they will not hold me up. I fall to the ground and slither like a snake into the garage and to the bottom of the basement stairs.

My legs are extremely swollen, and my head is pounding with the worst headache of my life. My vision is also beginning to get very blurry. After some very hard attempts to get up the steps by myself, I realize I just can't. Derinda gets behind me and helps push and pick up my legs, and very slowly we get me up two flights of steps into the living room. I lie on the floor in terrible pain, just trying to catch my breath. I really feel like I am going to die right there on the floor. I just cry, close my eyes, and rest for a while. She gives me pillows and helps get my dirty work clothes off me.

I truly don't know what I am going to do. I am in very bad shape now. It will be Monday before I go to the STAT Clinic at Kennestone Hospital in Marietta, Georgia.

I just rest. I can't take any more physical movement. I should call 911 and have an ambulance take me to the hospital that instant. Derinda wants to do just that. I constantly and very slowly shake my head no.

I do not remember much about the rest of this night other than knowing I can't lie on my left side at all, or I will choke to death. I can't breathe at all in that position. I begin to think that if I just sleep, I will feel a little better in the morning. I get her to help me drink some water, and I fall asleep in agonizing pain all over my body. It feels like there are small bombs are going off inside my head.

Saturday
October 27, 2018

I wake up around 6:00 AM. My legs feel a little better, and the swelling is almost gone. However, my head is still throbbing so badly that I can't hold it up straight. If I try to, I lose my vision, which feels almost like I am having a diabetic attack. I know it is not my diabetes causing my inability to talk and walk.

I am kind of hungry. I bang on the floor, and she wakes up and comes to check on me.

Together, we get me up on my feet, and I am actually able to stand long enough to get to the kitchen table and sit down in a chair. Thank God she is a strong woman, or I might still be lying on the cold hardwood floor. She makes coffee, but I can barely swallow it. This is a new issue; now I am practically choking just to swallow coffee. She is so scared that she is very nervous and crying, trying not to let me see her. I feel terrible. It really hurts me for her to have to see me in this sad and helpless condition. Whatever is wrong with me is so serious it literally is causing my entire body to shut down slowly and painfully.

I struggle through a breakfast bowl of oatmeal, milk, and coffee. Just eating zaps all my energy. I am physically tired again and need to sleep again, but first, I must make myself get to the restroom. I am able to stand up using the chair to help me get up. I then try to make my legs move, but they don't act right at all. My motor skills are very messed up, and I am wobbly like a baby learning to take its first steps. I do manage to get to the hall bath and use the facilities. I get to the bedroom and fall into the bed. She puts my legs up on the bed, and I fall fast asleep again.

CHAPTER 5

Monday
October 29 2018

I wake up after a very painful and restless night. It's hard to breathe, and I cannot move my legs at all without help. Derinda gets up to help me out of bed and into the shower. I shower, she helps me out of the shower, and I get dressed. Then we go to the doctor's appointment at the STAT Clinic at Kennestone Hospital. I am not feeling very good at all; I'm choking a lot and coughing up yellow liquid. When I cough, it hurts deep inside my body, and I can barely breathe. She helps me out of the house and down to the car. We get to the car and head to the hospital.

I am in a meeting with my cardiologist, Dr. Hiren. He asks me three questions, listens to my breathing, and says to me, "You are struggling to breathe, aren't you?"

I answer, "Yes, sir."

He says he would like to directly admit me into the hospital and begin some tests to see just what is causing all my recent illness.

Derinda and I both cry. She says, "Thank you. Yes, let's get things started right away."

The doctor sends a nurse for a wheelchair as I am so weak I just can't walk that far.

Derinda is really scared and upset, so I just hold her hand when I can, as I really can't talk well enough to be understood anymore. My voice has been taken from me at this point. I am so scared and so tired. When we get to the hospital, they put me in a semiprivate room. The man next to me and his wife are going through a rough spot also. I try to rest, but every twelve minutes or so, someone is coming in the room to check something on me or the other patient. It is hard to rest peacefully.

I am in so much pain I really am beginning to feel like I might be dying. I am not sure what is going to happen to me.

They take my blood and give me a breathing treatment. It helps a little, but I know I am not going home for a while. I am so weak I'm not able to even turn myself on my side in the bed without her help. They put an IV in my left hand for future use. It hurts like crazy from the get-go. They then tell me it will be needed for future blood draws and contrast for CT scans.

So we now know it is much more serious than I thought. I just don't know what is causing the knots in my neck and my inability to talk, walk, and stand on my own. I am told by the head nurse that it will be twenty-four hours before they have results and that the doctor will then know what is going on with me.

Derinda says she is staying with me. I just hold her hand tightly and don't let go. I want to just cry, but even that hurts. So I just close my eyes and lie there, thanking God she is by my side while all these people are poking and sticking things in me.

The patient next to me is loud, and his guest just never stops talking at all. He is an extremely long-winded person. I need sleep, but it is hopeless. I try to sleep as Derinda stays close by my side. She is all I've got now. I am in constant silent prayer with the good Lord to help me shake this illness and get back to normal. I am finally left alone long enough to drift off to sleep.

1:15 AM
October 30, 2018

Derinda is fast asleep already. All this has been absolutely frightening to her. I am her everything, and she is about to just fall apart. Derinda holds herself together as much as she can so as not to cause me any more pain. Seeing her cry only hurts me.

I think many prayers, and suddenly I am awakened by what I will call a vicious blood-sucking vampire, who, at three forty-five in the morning, is there to take a blood sample. I am truly struggling with all the strength I can muster to simply breathe as she takes my blood. Derinda wakes up and holds my hand. I can barely see as my eyes are swollen and very glassy. I just stare into her eyes and squeeze her hand tightly, crying myself back to sleep with tears trickling out of my eyes. I can't help it.

My body is telling me to get up, but it will not let me. I need to use the bathroom, so I tap her hand three times. That is how she knows I need to get up and go. This time she has to hold me up as I am not able to stand on my own at all. My legs don't work, and my back feels like someone is sticking a double-edged sword through my spine, at the tailbone area—excruciatingly painful. Derinda struggles to get me back to bed, but she manages. I get two more hours of sleep.

6:30 AM

They come in and get me on another gurney to take me down to the CT scan and MRI. Dr. Don Shaffer has called the head nurse and stated the scans are not good enough. He needs new ones and has ordered an MRI of my brain as well. As they wheel me out of my room, they tell me that once the MRI is done, I will be taken to my private room. The doctor will make his rounds at 10:00 AM, and I am first priority on his visits today. So that's good news.

I arrive at the MRI room, and two male nurses assist me off the gurney and onto the MRI table. The procedure takes about an hour. Then they help me off the table, into a wheelchair, and roll me out to the hallway. A young nurse comes to get me and takes me to the oncology floor here at Kennestone Hospital.

I get to my private room. It's now 7:45 AM. The knots in my throat area have gotten much bigger. It is now a very serious problem for me to breathe, and swallowing anything when I eat is very hard. They have my breakfast waiting for me, and I am so glad. My throat is so dry from the oral contrast solution. I need something to drink. Coffee will be great if I can swallow it without choking.

Derinda is sleeping in the chair beside my new, more comfortable bed. I know she is so tired and worried about me. I hate to wake her up, but I need her help to eat. So I use my cane to tap her arm lightly and wake her up. She is surprised, sees me, gets up, and hugs me. She opens my milk carton, puts butter and jelly on my bread, and assists me with eating my eggs, oatmeal, and bacon.

I now shake badly and have become so weak I can hardly hold the fork and get it into my mouth without food falling off. She asks me if it would be okay if she goes home for a bit to check on the dogs, take a shower, get some stuff, and come back. I'm not able to talk, so I just nod my head yes

A bunch of new people walk in my room at 8:40 AM. They are my new team of nurses. They introduce themselves, get my medicine list, and get me all hooked up to an IV machine and an oxygen machine. The oxygen is great; it helps me breathe without having to struggle.

Then they tell me I have to get insulin because the Metformin is not okay to mix with the other treatments I will be getting, so they give it to me in my stomach area. It burns at first, then it itches. I hate it but have no choice; I am diabetic and need my medication.

The head nurse, Chelsey, says, "Okay, that is all for a few hours. Your doctor will be in around 2:00 PM to discuss the new scans and MRI of your brain with you."

Derinda says, "Okay," and lets them know I can't talk and that they need to hand me my phone. She tells them that I can type answers to their questions, or they can get me a pen and paper. She advises the nurse staff she will be leaving shortly but will return before two.

Then the daytime vampire walks in. She wants more blood. I am beginning to wish I had a wooden stake. These blood takers always need a tube of blood at the most inconvenient times.

Derinda leaves, kisses me on my cheek, and tells me she loves me with tears in her eyes. I squeeze her hand and nod my head. It upsets me not to be able to say, "I love you too." I try, but it hurts too badly, and talking makes me choke.

I lie back in the bed and try to get some rest.

CHAPTER 6

Speech impaired; I think prayers of survival
_1:45_ PM

I awake to the sound of people talking. I look to my left and see Mitchel (my brother) and Derinda talking about me. I can barely see. The colors are not right; it's like I see in black and white—very weird. I hear people talking in the hallway. It is my doctor. He steps into my room; says, "Hello"; pulls up my chart; and begins to discuss what is wrong with me.

I am told I have small-cell lung cancer, a very large tumor in the left lung, a large tumor on two of my aorta's main valves to my heart, and several other large tumors in my stomach cavity. This explains the trouble I am having when I breathe. Then the doctor says I have over twenty lesions (small- to medium-size tumors) in my brain. He is very concerned about my brain and says we must begin treatment immediately.

I am in shock, but I nod my head. Derinda tells Dr. Shaffer I cannot really talk anymore, so nodding my head means I understand.

Then the doctor says, "I can't say you are curable because you are not, but you are *treatable*. We may have to do chemo and radiation at some point, but chemo for sure right away." He then explains there is nothing on earth currently in regular chemotherapy that will penetrate the brain.

I am very emotional. At this point, the doctor speaks of a new experimental immunotherapy chemo that has never before been given to a human for small-cell lung cancer, but he believes he can get the hospital to get it for me. I will have to sign papers to get this drug because it is not approved by the FDA yet, and insurance will not cover it. I ask the doctor if that's all there is, in his professional opinion, that he is aware of out there to help give me a fighting chance. If not, then okay, I will do it.

Dr. Shaffer holds my hand and says, "Okay, I will call them immediately, and your first round of chemo will begin at six tomorrow night. I am also going to have the radiation specialist come in and discuss radiation treatment options with you." Then he asks Derinda if I have a will.

She says, "No."

The doctor says that now would be a good time to start getting my affairs in order, that I am stage four, and that my diagnosis is one of the worst he has seen in a very long time.

With all that said, the doctor exits the room and, as he leaves, tells me that he has also ordered a bronchoscopy procedure to be done on my throat and a tissue sample to be taken to see exactly what is going on. They will do this at 4:30 PM today.

Derinda says, "Okay."

As the doctor leaves the room, my brother comes over to my bed and says, "Stay strong, Bubba. I lost Daddy and can't lose you too."

I get emotional again and am in more pain now than ever before in my life. With all my illnesses, now I am beginning to go blind, but I keep this to myself. Derinda comes over to my bed, crying and shaking. I lift up my hand; I am shaking and crying as well. She holds my hand tightly, and I squeeze her hand tight.

I am truly more scared than I have ever been before in my life. I know now I might just die here in this bed, and my chance of survival is very, very low. I can tell my body is shutting down. I silently pray to the *Lord* to give me His strength and come into my body and help me expel this wickedness.

Derinda says, "Jeff, please fight this with all you have in you. I can't lose you. I love you and need you to get well."

I just squeeze her and my brother's hands and continue to pray in my mind for God to give me healing.

I am very tired and thirsty, and my mouth is very dry. I can't eat because I am having surgery in two hours. Derinda gets the nurse to get me some ginger ale and ice water. I drink both, lay my head back onto the pillows, and, teary-eyed, fall asleep again. I am so tired and weak. I truly don't feel like I am strong enough to fight this off, but I have got to. I know I am weak, but *I am not gonna let this be the death of me*.

CHAPTER 7

I am very sick, tired all the time, and I can't talk well enough for anyone to understand me. I am thinking my prayers to God to help me. I am scared to go to sleep or even close my eyes, not knowing if I will be able to see when I awaken.

My brother and Derinda are both very concerned. Mitchel has to leave at 9:00 PM, while Derinda stays, too scared to leave my side. I am glad because I really feel as if I am going to die anytime now.

I am fighting this thing with all my strength, but at this point, it is not much. I muster up some energy, and while holding her hand, I fall asleep.

I am woken up by a nurse in the wee hours of the morning saying she needs to take my blood. They are keeping a very watchful eye on my white blood cell count, as the doctor needs them to be in a range acceptable for me to be treated after surgery. They will check again.

6:00 AM
October 31, 2018

I wake up in a lot of pain in my throat as they have already done the surgery. I was put under during the operation, and I really don't remember much. I can't eat, but I can drink water and eat applesauce. That is it. The nurse comes to check my vitals and tells me the doctor will be in to talk to me this morning before 9:00 AM about the results of the bronchoscopy and to discuss a treatment plan.

I turn on the TV and watch the morning news while she is still sleeping. I am trying not to wake her because she has not really slept well in three days.

The doctor walks in and says, "Good morning."

Derinda wakes up.

He says we are going to start chemotherapy tonight and continue for the next three days at five thirty every evening. I will be given four bags of chemo and one of immune therapy. It is all we can do, and if the treatment does not cause me to have a heart attack in the first round, we will continue. He explains that there is a very real probability the treatment itself will kill me. I have to sign a waiver form to receive the immune therapy because it is not yet approved for use in humans by the FDA. I am not really able to see or talk, so I nod my head.

Derinda says, "Wait a minute. What is this stuff that is not yet approved for use in people?"

Dr. Shaffer responds, "It is the only chemo known on earth to penetrate the brain. If we do not get the rapid growth of the twenty-plus tumors in his brain under control, he will be dead in days. This is the only drug with some clinical trials on large animals that has been effective. He asked me to find something that may have a chance to help him. I really believe this is the drug to do so. Jimmy Carter was given this drug, and it helped him. They are revising the version we are going to give Jeff. It will be much stronger. He will be the second person on earth to receive it and the first man to get it for small-cell carcinoma of the lung, which has spread into the brain, as it almost always does." Dr. Shaffer holds my hand and Derinda's hand. "We all need to pray."

I am in a fight for my life. He then says a prayer with us and leaves the room.

October 31, 2018

I have been sleeping, crying, and in serious pain all night long, with nurses looking in on me every hour. Derinda has been crying in the chair next to me and hasn't left my side except to get a cup of coffee. I am having a really hard time just breathing; it is now a truly challenging task. I am basically blind, can't talk at all, and can no longer pick up my legs on my own to get out of bed and use the bathroom.

I have to go about every three hours, and as much as it bothers me to wake her up, she has to get up and help me out of bed, holding me up on my left side. Then I can use my cane with my right hand. Yet I am barely able to go five feet around the corner to my bathroom. My legs are shaking, and it is becoming close to impossible for me to stand anymore. If she were not supporting one half of my body, I would simply fall to the ground like a dead leaf from an oak tree in the fall.

I realize this, and I know Derinda must as well. At this moment, she begins shaking and crying as much as I am but manages to get me back into bed. We both lie in my bed together for the rest of the night, as I feel like once I fall back to sleep, I am probably not going to wake up again. I am comforted by her body warmth and fall fast asleep.

6:15 AM
October31, 2018

Presurgery nurses come to prep me for my bronchoscopy. They take my vitals; my heart rate is very slow and my breathing is extremely weak. Again, they take my blood. I have big knots under my arms, and all my lymph nodes are bulging out in my throat. I truly look like Cousin Itt, the fictional character on *The Addams Family*. I am certain that everyone can see all this distortion but me, as I am totally in darkness now when my eyes are open.

I now feel death setting in for the first time in my forty-seven years of life. I am in constant prayer for God's grace to guide me through "the valley of the shadow of death" because I feel in all my body that death is knocking on the door.

Trapped in this absolutely pitiful situation, I just want to scream out, "Derinda, I love you!" but I can't even talk. It angers me. I am in a rage of fear and just angry with myself at this point for ever smoking cigarettes.

They wheel me out of the room and down the hall, with her holding my hand for a few feet. I squeeze her hand as tight as I can and wave bye to her, as I truly think that once they put me under for this procedure, I most likely will not ever wake back up. I feel terrified and am more scared than ever before in my life. I can only think prayers, like *God, please hold me in Your arms and wake me after this is done.* They give me my shot and ask me to count backward from ten to one, and that's the last thing I can remember until later that afternoon, around 4:30 PM.

I am woken up by my aunt's sweet voice. She had made it to the hospital and is holding my hand. I open my eyes but cannot see anything but darkness. My throat is hurting very badly as they had to remove some tissue. She continues holding my hand. It feels like my mother, her sister, is also there in my room with me. A very warm and safe feeling comes over my body. Then Derinda holds my other hand, and I hear a familiar voice in my room. It's my uncle Jack. I know then that I am alive, and I begin to get my bearings and surroundings back slowly. I thank God for His grace. I again want to scream out, "I love you all! I am so sorry you have to see me like this!" but I can't talk at all.

It truly just *sucks*.

CHAPTER 8

It is now time for me to say goodbye to all my visitors and get as much rest as I can before the next round of blood work is done. I finish up a bowl of Jell-O, a glass of water, and some apple juice. I wave to my family and drift off to sleep with Derinda by my side.

I guess you could say my family is very concerned about the current status of my diagnosis, and my prognosis is not good at all. I think my prayers as I drift in and out of consciousness.

3:45 AM
November 1, 2018

The vampire lady is in my room to take my blood again. I wake up. She sticks me and gets three tubes of blood. Now I cannot go back to sleep. I just lie there and think of my life and all those I remember—all the good times, like the times with my brother going fishing in the river, playing baseball, and riding bikes. I think more prayers, and the door opens. It's my breakfast.

Derinda wakes up and helps me sit up in bed and eat. We are patiently waiting for Dr. Shaffer to come in and give us the news of the biopsy results and a layout of the treatment plan. At 9:00 AM, he walks in and tells me it is small-cell lung cancer that has spread into my brain, as it almost always does in smokers. This is the cause of my vision and voice impairment. All my lymph nodes are swollen because of cancer rapidly spreading through my blood and throughout my body.

Dr. Shaffer tells me there is no regular chemotherapy currently known to penetrate the brain. However, there is a non-FDA-approved, brand-new immune therapy drug in very early experimental trials that has proven to be very effective in large animals. If I sign a waiver, he thinks he can get the hospital to help get it to try in me.

The doctor says we will, at some point, have a regimen of radiation to my brain to help get the lesions under control. We will begin therapy tonight with five different dosages, and the sixth one will be the immune therapy tomorrow. He then says, "This treatment is very risky, and your chance of survival is only 2 percent. With all the dosages of chemo, your odds will be reduced to just a 1 percent chance."

He says that I will get very sick and become much weaker and that special attention will need to be focused on my heart functions. The good news is my heart is strong. I thank him by shaking his hand and nodding my head. I squeeze his hand tight before I let it go, and he exits, saying, "I will return in two days. We will then see how you are accepting the therapy, as it takes forty-eight hours for it to really start attacking the cancer cells in the body."

By this time, I am shaking in complete and utter fear. *I am dying.* Both Derinda and I get emotional. She is even more scared than I am, as I am pretty much her everything in life, as she is mine. I hold her tightly, and we cry ourselves to sleep.

At 5:00 AM, the head nurse steps in with the first round of chemo and tells me it will take five hours to administer all six dosages.

And so it begins.

*****

When I wake up at 4:00 PM, the nurse gives me a shot that puts me out for my biopsy throat surgery at 4:30 PM. They then roll me down the hall, and out I go.

Later that evening, I wake up and am back in my room. My throat hurts terribly. I can't have any solid food for a day or so because of internal stitches down in my throat, so Jell-O and water it is. I am so sick I really am not able to eat much anyway. My aunt and wife are in my room, watching over me like my mother would be if she were alive. I really miss my mother and know her eyes are looking down from heaven, watching all these doctors' and nurses' every move.

I am just a very lucky man to have family, friends, coworkers, cousins, and so many people in churches across the planet praying for me. I have learned in the last few hours how absolutely precious everything in life is, especially the ability to breathe on my own. I am not currently able to breathe in the proper amount of oxygen without it being pumped through hoses in my nose. I can definitely tell you all that smoking is the stupidity in my life. Absolutely, it has almost killed me. I have lost my mobility in my legs, and my sight is fading to darkness. My ability to talk is so badly impaired that even if I spoke, you could not understand what I was saying. The throat biopsy has not helped that at all.

I am just a bag of bones lying in a bed, fighting for every breath. I truly cannot function as a man. It is the worst thing in life to just lie in a bed thinking about the person I love the most in life—my wife. I am not able to see her, kiss her, or speak to her. All of this is just making me so sad. I only have myself to blame for what I am going through and can honestly say, "I feel half dead, and for the first time in my life, I am not in control." I need loved ones and Derinda now more than ever. God is my only way through this. My doctors are all very intelligent, but they are very limited in what they can do for me. And I am so sick it is a race against time to get treated with chemo or radiation. This is the decision that all the doctors are trying to figure out.

I am in their hands and am scared to sleep now, as I think I may not be strong enough to wake up again. I am trying not to let my family know or tell them that's how I really feel, that I know I am not as tough as I think I am. In all, it is just embarrassing to be in such pitiful shape. *Love will keep me alive—* this is my thought as I give in to exhaustion and drift off to sleep. My final thoughts are of my daughters, whom I love with all my heart, as well as Derinda and my brothers. I ask for God to please accept my soul and guide me through the night.

CHAPTER 9

Going forward, after getting out of the hospital and going home, I spend the next hundred days at my house recovering from chemotherapy treatments. During this time, all my hair falls out, and I become very sick. I visit the oncology lab every twenty-one days to receive a new dose of chemotherapy. It is the immunotherapy medication Atezolizumab. After two treatments of the Atezolizumab, my body adjusts to the chemo, and it doesn't make me sick anymore—thank goodness.

I am very weak from all of this and cannot do a whole lot; I just stay on the couch in my house, watching television and sleeping. I spend a lot of time saying my prayers, hoping I get better soon so I can go back to work and continue to pay for my house.

As the months roll by, the immunotherapy is really doing wonders for me. There are at least two times when I know that I fall asleep while I choking. This is a frightening experience because I completely pass out from no breath. I'm very fortunate to own a little wiry-haired terrier. She has taken it upon herself to get on top of my chest and lick me in the face until I open my eyes both times. I guess you could say she's my savior. She's just one more humbling reminder of why I have to live and survive this.

Somewhere around my fifteenth immuno-therapy treatment, while visiting my doctor that morning, I'm told that one of the tumors in my brain has started growing rapidly, and now I need to have radiation shot through my brain. So I schedule the appointment. I am not looking forward to this and was hoping I never would have to go down that road. Life is a long and winding road that will take you on many trips. What I have learned is that no matter what, somehow you get backed into a corner, and it seems as if there's no way out of that corner. There truly isn't without faith in God.

On my first trip to the radiation doctor's office, they fit me with this mask that goes around my head. I'm lying on a metal table. They strap my head to the table and bring this mesh-looking thing out, then push it gently over my face. It conforms to the exact shape of my face. They use a Sharpie to mark the spots on my brain. This is what will strap me to the table when I'm in the machine that shoots the gamma rays through my brain. So I do seven days' worth of radiation treatments. It equaled eleven thousand gamma rays shot through my brain. Six weeks later, they do more CT scans of my upper torso and my brain.

On my next trip to the doctor, they read my results to me and say that the radiation treatment was effective. I no longer have any cancers growing in my head or in my upper torso. So for anyone going through something like this, this is proof that medicine, good doctors, and prayer are very helpful. We've all at least been to some form of church in our lifetime and heard the preacher say you have to believe in the Lord to receive the Lord's blessing. I am living, breathing proof of that.

AFTERWORD

I continue on my journey with treatments for the next two years, receiving the immune therapy. I am now back to work and living my life as best as I can. I do all the things I always have; it's just that I move a little slower. I use dollies or hand trucks to move heavier items in my construction job as a superintendent. I am in full remission and only go to get CT scans two more times in 2020. I am not ever going to be as strong as I once was, but I am still able to live a normal life with my spouse and work. I now only have to be very careful and watchful of people with COVID-19. I get all my shots to prevent the coronavirus and all its variants because of the pandemic.

Luckily, as a contractor for McDonald's Corporation, I am able to continue working right through all of the pandemic, never missing a paycheck. This is a blessing, especially since I now have $79,000 worth of medical bills to pay between the two cancer-treatment hospital facilities treating me.

I have now built ten more buildings for my company and am doing amazingly well health-wise. I think I am going to be okay. It is now mid-September 2023. I am approaching my five-year mark and am no longer doing scans or any treatments. Every single day, I hit my knees and praise the Lord for my blessings. I strongly encourage all of you out there who might be going through something similar to stay the course. Do not ever give in, no matter how sick you get from treatments. Stand up to "CANCER." It is a very mean demon. With the will and desire to continue living and God as the leader of your journey, you can beat this and move through it.

With all this said, I would like to thank anyone who finds this helpful in their struggle for taking the time to read my story of all the milestones passed and miracles received.

ABOUT THE AUTHOR

Jeff is mid aged and works as a commercial contractor. He has built all types of restaurants, retail stores, and various other commercial buildings all over the southern states. He really enjoys his time off with family or simply doing nothing. He is very fond of camping, boating, fishing, hunting, and cooking on the grill. People have said that he is rough around the edges but soft at heart, and he is known to be hard-headed and demanding but to the point. Jeff is a very hardworking man.

When a life-threatening event happened at just forty-seven years old, Jeff felt a calling to pick up his pen and paper, put the tools away, and share his story with the world. He firmly believes that the great doctors, family, coworkers, friends, and many people praying for him to pull through stage-four small-cell carcinoma is the reason God used His healing hands to bring him through the pain. He truly learned you must believe to receive. All things are possible if you have faith. God let him live to share this story with all who are facing death head-on. Stand up to cancer; you can beat it.

He still works hard today and does what he loves—building buildings. He does things a bit slower now but still gets projects done on time. He has been blessed to work for a great company for many years, and it keeps him busy. No amount of work will ever harm a person; it only keeps you up and fighting. Oh yeah, Benjamins are nice as well. He gets to do things with the money that he works so hard for that give him peace of mind and joy.

Fighting cancer is no joke. Yes, it is extremely costly. Even with insurance, you still get hit with outrageous bills, deductibles, and so forth. He learned that it is just part of it if you want to live. Well, in hopes that all who fear the worst is near, he asks that you hear his story and choose life. It's worth it. Fight you must. Chemotherapy is very hard. Immunotherapies are not as bad but will save your life. He bids Godspeed to all who are in the fight!